AF711113

TAX DEDUCTIONS A to Z™ Log Book

Anne Skalka, CPA

with Janice Beth Gregg

TAX DEDUCTIONS A TO Z™ LOG BOOK

Copyright © 2006
Boxed Books Inc.
All rights reserved.
No part of this book shall be reproduced, stored in a retrieval system, or transmitted by any means, electronic, mechanical, photocopying, recording, or otherwise, without written permission from the publisher.

• *For information* •
Boxed Books
19 Woodlane Rd.
Lawrenceville NJ 08648
www.boxedbooks.com
• *Produced by* •
Boxed Books Inc.,
Lawrenceville, NJ

•*Layout & Illustration by* •
Michael Wilson

International Standard Book Number:
978-1-933672-19-9
Library of Congress Control Number: 2006906770

Printed in the USA

Boxed Books titles are available at special discounts for bulk purchases by corporations, institutions, and other organizations. For more information, please contact the Publisher, Boxed Books, Inc., 19 Woodlane Road, Lawrenceville, NJ

DISCLAIMER OF WARRANTY/LIMIT OF LIABILITY

The information contained in this book is for general guidance on matters of interest only. The application and impact of laws can vary widely based on the specific facts involved. Given the changing nature of laws, rules, and regulations, there may be delays, omissions or inaccuracies in information contained herein. Accordingly, the information is provided with the understanding that the authors and publishers are not herein engaged in rendering legal, accounting, tax, or other professional advice and services. As such, it should not be used as a substitute for consultation with professional accounting, tax, legal or other competent advisers.

A PRAYER FOR THE IRS

Oh, Internal Revenue Service,
ruler of all Washington,
We sanctify thee, as thou
goest about thy business,
enthroned by the glory of Congress
and the powers of section 7801 of the
Internal Revenue Code.

Have mercy on thy servants,
oh mighty Department of the Treasury,
and forgive us our hallowed deductions.
Deliver us from the grasp of the statutory
authority of the revenue auditor,
and lead us into the promised land
of the everlasting refund.

AUTOMOBILE EXPENSE

If you own your car and use it exclusively in your job or business, then the entire cost of operating it can be deducted from taxable income.

The deduction can be based on either miles driven or the actual cost of maintaining and operating the car, including registration and licensing fees, insurance, gas, maintenance and repairs, tires, garage rental, parking fees, tolls, and depreciation.

The deduction for the business use of your personal car depends on whether you are an employee or are self-employed. If you are self-employed, the cost relating to the business use of your personal car may be deducted from self-employment income as a business expense.

If the car is not exclusively used for business purposes, the deductible amount is prorated to reflect this. If you are an employee the job-related use of your personal car is treated as a miscellaneous expense, subject to the 2% AGI threshold.

Automobile expenses associated with medical travel, charitable travel, job search, and other tax deductible activities may also be deducted. Self-employed individuals can deduct work-related costs directly from self-employment income.

EXPENSES WHICH MAY BE DEDUCTIBLE

The state **registration** fee for your personal car may be tax deductible if it is an annual fee based on the car's value. Some states base their automobile registration fees on factors like weight, model, vehicle age, or engine size. Those fees are not deductible.

The cost to **lease** a car that is used in tax deductible activities (i.e., travel that is related to work, charitable activities, medical treatment, or a job search) may be partly or wholly tax deductible. There are restrictions on the cost calculations for the lease, and limits on the amount of depreciation that can be deducted.

If you own or lease a car and use it in tax deductible activities, then the **operating costs** can be deducted from taxes. The deduction can be based on either miles driven, using the IRS standard mileage allowance, or the actual costs of maintaining and operating the car. If the deduction is based on actual costs, you may include the cost of **gasoline** or other **fuel**, **licensing fees, insurance, maintenance** and **repairs, tires, garage rental, parking fees, tolls**, and **depreciation.** There are restrictions on the cost calculations for leased cars, and limits on the amount of depreciation that can be deducted.

The costs associated with use of a car are tax deductible as a **medical expense** if traveling for a doctor's appointment or medical treatment, to obtain prescription drugs, to attend AA meetings, or to attend a medical conference on a relevant illness or condition.

If the car is not exclusively used for business or other tax deductible purposes, the deductible amount is prorated to reflect the portion of personal use.

EXPENSES WHICH MAY BE DEDUCTIBLE

The state **registration** fee for your personal car may be tax deductible if it is an annual fee based on the car's value. Some states base their automobile registration fees on factors like weight, model, vehicle age, or engine size. Those fees are not deductible.

The cost to **lease** a car that is used in tax deductible activities (i.e. travel that is related to work, charitable activities, medical treatment, or a job search) may be partly or wholly tax deductible. There are restrictions on the cost calculations for the lease, and limits on the amount of depreciation that can be deducted.

If you own or lease a car and use it in tax deductible activities, then the **operating costs** can be deducted from taxes. The deduction can be based on either miles driven, using the IRS standard mileage allowance, or the actual costs of maintaining and operating the car. If the deduction is based on actual costs, you may include the cost of **gasoline** or other **fuel**, **licensing fees, insurance, maintenance** and **repairs, tires, garage rental, parking fees, tolls**, and **depreciation.** There are restrictions on the cost calculations for leased cars, and limits on the amount of depreciation that can be deducted.

The costs associated with use of a car are tax deductible as a **medical expense** if traveling for a doctor's appointment or medical treatment, to obtain prescription drugs, to attend AA meetings, or to attend a medical conference on a relevant illness or condition.

If the car is not exclusively used for business or other tax deductible purposes, the deductible amount is prorated to reflect the portion of personal use.

EXPENSES WHICH MAY BE DEDUCTIBLE

The state **registration** fee for your personal car may be tax deductible if it is an annual fee based on the car's value. Some states base their automobile registration fees on factors like weight, model, vehicle age, or engine size. Those fees are not deductible.

The cost to **lease** a car that is used in tax deductible activities (i.e. travel that is related to work, charitable activities, medical treatment, or a job search) may be partly or wholly tax deductible. There are restrictions on the cost calculations for the lease, and limits on the amount of depreciation that can be deducted.

If you own or lease a car and use it in tax deductible activities, then the **operating costs** can be deducted from taxes. The deduction can be based on either miles driven, using the IRS standard mileage allowance, or the actual costs of maintaining and operating the car. If the deduction is based on actual costs, you may include the cost of **gasoline** or other **fuel**, **licensing fees, insurance, maintenance** and **repairs, tires, garage rental, parking fees, tolls**, and **depreciation.** There are restrictions on the cost calculations for leased cars, and limits on the amount of depreciation that can be deducted.

The costs associated with use of a car are tax deductible as a **medical expense** if traveling for a doctor's appointment or medical treatment, to obtain prescription drugs, to attend AA meetings, or to attend a medical conference on a relevant illness or condition.

If the car is not exclusively used for business or other tax deductible purposes, the deductible amount is prorated to reflect the portion of personal use.

DATE • ____ / ____ / ____

START MILEAGE	*END MILEAGE*	*TRIP*

Gas •	*Tolls* •

VEHICLE • ______________________________

DESTINATION	*PURPOSE*

Parking •	*Repairs •*

TOTAL DEDUCTIBLE MILEAGE •

DATE • ____ / ____ / ____

START MILEAGE	END MILEAGE	TRIP

Gas •	Tolls •

VEHICLE • ____________________

DESTINATION	PURPOSE

Parking •	Repairs •

TOTAL DEDUCTIBLE MILEAGE •

DATE • ____ / ____ / ____

START MILEAGE	*END MILEAGE*	*TRIP*

Gas •	*Tolls* •

MILEAGE TRACKER

VEHICLE • ______________________________

DESTINATION	*PURPOSE*

Parking •	*Repairs •*

TOTAL DEDUCTIBLE MILEAGE •

DATE • ____ / ____ / ____

START MILEAGE	END MILEAGE	TRIP

Gas •

Tolls •

MILEAGE TRACKER

VEHICLE • ______________________________

DESTINATION	*PURPOSE*

Parking •	*Repairs* •

TOTAL DEDUCTIBLE MILEAGE •

DATE • ____ / ____ / ____

START MILEAGE	END MILEAGE	TRIP

Gas •	Tolls •

VEHICLE • ______________________

DESTINATION	PURPOSE

Parking •	Repairs •

TOTAL DEDUCTIBLE MILEAGE •

DATE • ____ / ____ / ____

START MILEAGE	END MILEAGE	TRIP

Gas •	Tolls •

MILEAGE TRACKER

VEHICLE • ____________________

DESTINATION	PURPOSE

Parking •

Repairs •

TOTAL DEDUCTIBLE MILEAGE •

DATE • ____ / ____ / ____

START MILEAGE	END MILEAGE	TRIP

Gas •

Tolls •

VEHICLE •

DESTINATION	PURPOSE

Parking •	Repairs •

TOTAL DEDUCTIBLE MILEAGE •

DATE • ____ / ____ / ____

START MILEAGE	END MILEAGE	TRIP

Gas • | Tolls •

MILEAGE TRACKER

VEHICLE • ______________________________

DESTINATION	*PURPOSE*

Parking •	*Repairs •*

TOTAL DEDUCTIBLE MILEAGE •

DATE • ____ / ____ / ____

START MILEAGE	*END MILEAGE*	*TRIP*

Gas •	Tolls •

MILEAGE TRACKER

VEHICLE •

DESTINATION	PURPOSE

Parking •	Repairs •

TOTAL DEDUCTIBLE MILEAGE •

DATE • ____ / ____ / ____

START MILEAGE	*END MILEAGE*	*TRIP*

Gas •

Tolls •

MILEAGE TRACKER

VEHICLE • ______________________

DESTINATION	PURPOSE

Parking •	Repairs •

TOTAL DEDUCTIBLE MILEAGE •

DATE • ____ / ____ / ____

START MILEAGE	END MILEAGE	TRIP

Gas •

Tolls •

VEHICLE • ______________________

DESTINATION	*PURPOSE*

Parking •	*Repairs •*

TOTAL DEDUCTIBLE MILEAGE •

DATE • ____ / ____ / ____

START MILEAGE	END MILEAGE	TRIP

Gas •	Tolls •

MILEAGE TRACKER

VEHICLE • ______________________________

DESTINATION	*PURPOSE*

Parking •	*Repairs •*

TOTAL DEDUCTIBLE MILEAGE •

DATE • ____ / ____ / ____

START MILEAGE	END MILEAGE	TRIP

Gas •

Tolls •

VEHICLE • ______________________

DESTINATION	*PURPOSE*

Parking •	*Repairs •*

TOTAL DEDUCTIBLE MILEAGE •

DATE • ____ / ____ / ____

START MILEAGE	*END MILEAGE*	*TRIP*

Gas • *Tolls •*

MILEAGE TRACKER

VEHICLE • ____________________

DESTINATION	*PURPOSE*

Parking •	*Repairs •*

TOTAL DEDUCTIBLE MILEAGE •

DATE • ____ / ____ / ____

START MILEAGE	END MILEAGE	TRIP

Gas •

Tolls •

MILEAGE TRACKER

VEHICLE • ______________________________

DESTINATION	*PURPOSE*

Parking •	*Repairs •*

TOTAL DEDUCTIBLE MILEAGE •

DATE • ____ / ____ / ____

START MILEAGE	END MILEAGE	TRIP

Gas •

Tolls •

MILEAGE TRACKER

VEHICLE •

DESTINATION	*PURPOSE*

Parking •	*Repairs •*

TOTAL DEDUCTIBLE MILEAGE •

DATE • ____ / ____ / ____

START MILEAGE	END MILEAGE	TRIP

Gas •	Tolls •

VEHICLE • ______________________

DESTINATION	PURPOSE

Parking •	Repairs •

TOTAL DEDUCTIBLE MILEAGE •

DATE • ____ / ____ / ____

START MILEAGE	END MILEAGE	TRIP

Gas • | Tolls •

VEHICLE • ____________________

DESTINATION	PURPOSE

Parking •	Repairs •

TOTAL DEDUCTIBLE MILEAGE •

DATE • ____ / ____ / ____

START MILEAGE	*END MILEAGE*	*TRIP*

Gas •	Tolls •

MILEAGE TRACKER

VEHICLE • ______________________________

DESTINATION	PURPOSE

Parking •

Repairs •

TOTAL DEDUCTIBLE MILEAGE •

DATE • ____ / ____ / ____

START MILEAGE	*END MILEAGE*	*TRIP*

Gas •	Tolls •

VEHICLE • ______________________

DESTINATION	PURPOSE

Parking •	Repairs •

TOTAL DEDUCTIBLE MILEAGE •

DATE • ___ / ___ / ___

START MILEAGE	*END MILEAGE*	*TRIP*

Gas •	*Tolls* •

MILEAGE TRACKER

VEHICLE • ______________________

DESTINATION	*PURPOSE*

Parking •	*Repairs •*

TOTAL DEDUCTIBLE MILEAGE •

DATE • ____ / ____ / ____

START MILEAGE	END MILEAGE	TRIP

Gas •	Tolls •

VEHICLE •

DESTINATION	*PURPOSE*

Parking •	*Repairs •*

TOTAL DEDUCTIBLE MILEAGE •

DATE • ____ / ____ / ____

START MILEAGE	END MILEAGE	TRIP

Gas •

Tolls •

MILEAGE TRACKER

VEHICLE • ______________________

DESTINATION	*PURPOSE*

Parking •	*Repairs •*

TOTAL DEDUCTIBLE MILEAGE •

DATE • ____ / ____ / ____

START MILEAGE	*END MILEAGE*	*TRIP*

Gas •	Tolls •

MILEAGE TRACKER

VEHICLE • ______________________

DESTINATION	*PURPOSE*

Parking •	*Repairs* •

TOTAL DEDUCTIBLE MILEAGE •

DATE • ____ / ____ / ____

START MILEAGE	END MILEAGE	TRIP

Gas •	Tolls •

VEHICLE • ______________________

DESTINATION	*PURPOSE*

Parking •	*Repairs •*

TOTAL DEDUCTIBLE MILEAGE •

DATE • ____ / ____ / ____

START MILEAGE	*END MILEAGE*	*TRIP*

Gas •	*Tolls* •

MILEAGE TRACKER

VEHICLE • ______________________

DESTINATION	*PURPOSE*

Parking •	*Repairs •*

TOTAL DEDUCTIBLE MILEAGE •

DATE • ____ / ____ / ____

START MILEAGE	END MILEAGE	TRIP

Gas • Tolls •

VEHICLE • ______________________

DESTINATION	*PURPOSE*

Parking •	*Repairs •*

TOTAL DEDUCTIBLE MILEAGE •

DATE • ____ / ____ / ____

START MILEAGE	*END MILEAGE*	*TRIP*

Gas •	*Tolls •*

MILEAGE TRACKER

VEHICLE • ____________________

DESTINATION	*PURPOSE*

Parking •	*Repairs •*

TOTAL DEDUCTIBLE MILEAGE •

DATE • ____ / ____ / ____

START MILEAGE	END MILEAGE	TRIP

Gas •	Tolls •

VEHICLE •

DESTINATION	*PURPOSE*

Parking •	*Repairs* •

TOTAL DEDUCTIBLE MILEAGE •

DATE • ____ / ____ / ____

START MILEAGE	END MILEAGE	TRIP

Gas •

Tolls •

MILEAGE TRACKER

VEHICLE • ______________________

DESTINATION	*PURPOSE*

Parking •	*Repairs •*

TOTAL DEDUCTIBLE MILEAGE •

DATE • ____ / ____ / ____

START MILEAGE	END MILEAGE	TRIP

Gas •

Tolls •

VEHICLE •

DESTINATION	PURPOSE

Parking •	Repairs •

TOTAL DEDUCTIBLE MILEAGE •

DATE • ____ / ____ / ____

START MILEAGE	*END MILEAGE*	*TRIP*

Gas •	Tolls •

MILEAGE TRACKER

VEHICLE • ______________________________

DESTINATION	*PURPOSE*

Parking • *Repairs •*

TOTAL DEDUCTIBLE MILEAGE •

DATE • ____ / ____ / ____

START MILEAGE	END MILEAGE	TRIP

Gas •	Tolls •

MILEAGE TRACKER

VEHICLE • ______________________

DESTINATION	*PURPOSE*

Parking •	*Repairs* •

TOTAL DEDUCTIBLE MILEAGE •

DATE • ____ / ____ / ____

START MILEAGE	END MILEAGE	TRIP

Gas •	Tolls •

MILEAGE TRACKER

VEHICLE • ______________________

DESTINATION	*PURPOSE*

Parking •	*Repairs •*

TOTAL DEDUCTIBLE MILEAGE •

DATE • ____ / ____ / ____

START MILEAGE	END MILEAGE	TRIP

Gas •	Tolls •

MILEAGE TRACKER

VEHICLE • ______________________

DESTINATION	*PURPOSE*

Parking •	*Repairs •*

TOTAL DEDUCTIBLE MILEAGE •

DATE • ____ / ____ / ____

START MILEAGE	*END MILEAGE*	*TRIP*

Gas •	*Tolls •*

MILEAGE TRACKER

VEHICLE • ______________________

DESTINATION	PURPOSE

Parking •	Repairs •

TOTAL DEDUCTIBLE MILEAGE •

DATE • ____ / ____ / ____

START MILEAGE	*END MILEAGE*	*TRIP*

Gas •	*Tolls •*

VEHICLE • ______________________________

DESTINATION	*PURPOSE*

Parking •	*Repairs •*

TOTAL DEDUCTIBLE MILEAGE •

DATE • ____ / ____ / ____

START MILEAGE	*END MILEAGE*	*TRIP*

Gas •	*Tolls* •

MILEAGE TRACKER

VEHICLE • ______________________________

DESTINATION	*PURPOSE*

Parking •	*Repairs •*

TOTAL DEDUCTIBLE MILEAGE •

TRAVEL, ENTERTAINMENT, & MEALS

The business travel, entertainment and meals deduction includes the cost of all transportation between your home and your business destination, as well as local transportation once your destination is reached and a deduction for the cost of dining and entertaining business associates. You can use your actual dining costs or base the deduction on the IRS standard meal allowance established for your destination. In either case, the deduction is limited to 50% of the cost, and documentation and substantiation are required. The tax deduction for business travel may be limited by the regularity and duration of the travel. If you remain on site for the duration of your workweek, returning home on weekends, your travel to and from the work location and your weekday living expenses may not be tax deductible. It can be determined that you and your spouse have different tax homes for travel purposes, even though you maintain a single primary residence together. If a business trip is extended an extra day to take advantage of reduced airfare, the cost of the extra meals and lodging is also tax deductible, after applying the 50% limit to meal costs.

For the meals and entertainment deduction, you can use your actual dining costs or base the deduction on the IRS standard meal allowance established for your destination. In either case, the deduction is limited to 50% of the cost, and documentation and substantiation are required. Travel that directly benefits your volunteer service or other charitable activities is deductible as a charitable donation, subject to the limitations of that category of deductions.

EXPENSES WHICH MAY BE DEDUCTIBLE

Transportation between your home and your business destination, as well as local transportation once your destination is reached, and travel between work sites are all deductible. This can include **automobile expenses**—your own or a rental car—as well as bus, train, cab, and airfare, plus tips.

Your **meals** as well as expenses for business-related entertaining are deductible when traveling away from home. When hosting business associates, the meals must directly relate to the conducting of business, or precede or follow a business discussion. You can use your actual dining costs, or base the deduction on the IRS standard meal allowance. In either case, the deduction is limited to 50% of the cost. Entertaining business associates in your home also qualifies for this deduction, subject to the same conditions and limitations as outside events.

Conferences, conventions, trade shows, and **seminars** are deductible if you can document their benefit to your trade or business. Attendance fees, travel, lodging, and 50% of meal costs can be included in this deduction.

Lodging costs are deductible for overnight travel.

Miscellaneous travel expenses are tax deductible, such as laundry, dry cleaning, and other incidental expenses, including associated tips, after you have met the deduction threshold of 2% of your AGI (adjusted gross income). Self-employed individuals can deduct these types of expenses directly from self-employment income.

LOCATION • ______________________ | *Date* • / /

Attendees •

Notes •

Total • $ __________

LOCATION • ______________________ | *Date* • / /

Attendees •

Notes •

Total • $ __________

LOCATION • ______________________ | *Date* • / /

Attendees •

Notes •

Total • $ __________

LOCATION • ______________________ | *Date* • / /

Attendees •

Notes •

Total • $ __________

LOCATION • ______________________ | *Date* • / /

Attendees •

Notes •

Total • $ __________

LOCATION • ______________________ Date • / /

Attendees •

Notes •

Total • $ __________

LOCATION • ______________________ Date • / /

Attendees •

Notes •

Total • $ __________

LOCATION • ______________________ Date • / /

Attendees •

Notes •

Total • $ __________

LOCATION • ______________________ Date • / /

Attendees •

Notes •

Total • $ __________

LOCATION • ______________________ Date • / /

Attendees •

Notes •

Total • $ __________

LOCATION • ____________________ *Date* • / /

Attendees •

Notes •

Total • $ __________

LOCATION • ____________________ *Date* • / /

Attendees •

Notes •

Total • $ __________

LOCATION • ____________________ *Date* • / /

Attendees •

Notes •

Total • $ __________

LOCATION • ____________________ *Date* • / /

Attendees •

Notes •

Total • $ __________

LOCATION • ____________________ *Date* • / /

Attendees •

Notes •

Total • $ __________

TRAVEL, ENTERTAINMENT, & MEALS

LOCATION • ____________________ *Date* • / /

Attendees •

Notes •

Total • $ __________

LOCATION • ____________________ *Date* • / /

Attendees •

Notes •

Total • $ __________

LOCATION • ____________________ *Date* • / /

Attendees •

Notes •

Total • $ __________

LOCATION • ____________________ *Date* • / /

Attendees •

Notes •

Total • $ __________

LOCATION • ____________________ *Date* • / /

Attendees •

Notes •

Total • $ __________

LOCATION • ____________________ Date • / /

Attendees •

Notes •

Total • $ __________

LOCATION • ____________________ Date • / /

Attendees •

Notes •

Total • $ __________

LOCATION • ____________________ Date • / /

Attendees •

Notes •

Total • $ __________

LOCATION • ____________________ Date • / /

Attendees •

Notes •

Total • $ __________

LOCATION • ____________________ Date • / /

Attendees •

Notes •

Total • $ __________

TRAVEL, ENTERTAINMENT, & MEALS

LOCATION • ____________________ Date • / /

Attendees •

Notes •

Total • $ __________

LOCATION • ____________________ Date • / /

Attendees •

Notes •

Total • $ __________

LOCATION • ____________________ Date • / /

Attendees •

Notes •

Total • $ __________

LOCATION • ____________________ Date • / /

Attendees •

Notes •

Total • $ __________

LOCATION • ____________________ Date • / /

Attendees •

Notes •

Total • $ __________

LOCATION • ____________________ Date • / /

Attendees •

Notes •

Total • $ __________

LOCATION • ____________________ Date • / /

Attendees •

Notes •

Total • $ __________

LOCATION • ____________________ Date • / /

Attendees •

Notes •

Total • $ __________

LOCATION • ____________________ Date • / /

Attendees •

Notes •

Total • $ __________

LOCATION • ____________________ Date • / /

Attendees •

Notes •

Total • $ __________

TRAVEL, ENTERTAINMENT, & MEALS

LOCATION • ____________________ Date • / /

Attendees •

Notes •

Total • $ __________

LOCATION • ____________________ Date • / /

Attendees •

Notes •

Total • $ __________

LOCATION • ____________________ Date • / /

Attendees •

Notes •

Total • $ __________

LOCATION • ____________________ Date • / /

Attendees •

Notes •

Total • $ __________

LOCATION • ____________________ Date • / /

Attendees •

Notes •

Total • $ __________

LOCATION • ____________________ | Date • / /

Attendees •

Notes •

Total • $ __________

LOCATION • ____________________ | Date • / /

Attendees •

Notes •

Total • $ __________

LOCATION • ____________________ | Date • / /

Attendees •

Notes •

Total • $ __________

LOCATION • ____________________ | Date • / /

Attendees •

Notes •

Total • $ __________

LOCATION • ____________________ | Date • / /

Attendees •

Notes •

Total • $ __________

TRAVEL, ENTERTAINMENT, & MEALS

LOCATION • ______________________ *Date* • / /

Attendees •

Notes •

Total • $ __________

LOCATION • ______________________ *Date* • / /

Attendees •

Notes •

Total • $ __________

LOCATION • ______________________ *Date* • / /

Attendees •

Notes •

Total • $ __________

LOCATION • ______________________ *Date* • / /

Attendees •

Notes •

Total • $ __________

LOCATION • ______________________ *Date* • / /

Attendees •

Notes •

Total • $ __________

LOCATION • ______________ *Date* • / /

Attendees •

Notes •

Total • $ __________

LOCATION • ______________ *Date* • / /

Attendees •

Notes •

Total • $ __________

LOCATION • ______________ *Date* • / /

Attendees •

Notes •

Total • $ __________

LOCATION • ______________ *Date* • / /

Attendees •

Notes •

Total • $ __________

LOCATION • ______________ *Date* • / /

Attendees •

Notes •

Total • $ __________

TRAVEL, ENTERTAINMENT, & MEALS

LOCATION • ______________________ *Date* • / /

Attendees •

Notes •

Total • $ __________

LOCATION • ______________________ *Date* • / /

Attendees •

Notes •

Total • $ __________

LOCATION • ______________________ *Date* • / /

Attendees •

Notes •

Total • $ __________

LOCATION • ______________________ *Date* • / /

Attendees •

Notes •

Total • $ __________

LOCATION • ______________________ *Date* • / /

Attendees •

Notes •

Total • $ __________

LOCATION • ______________________ | Date • / /

Attendees •

Notes •

Total • $ __________

LOCATION • ______________________ | Date • / /

Attendees •

Notes •

Total • $ __________

LOCATION • ______________________ | Date • / /

Attendees •

Notes •

Total • $ __________

LOCATION • ______________________ | Date • / /

Attendees •

Notes •

Total • $ __________

LOCATION • ______________________ | Date • / /

Attendees •

Notes •

Total • $ __________

TRAVEL, ENTERTAINMENT, & MEALS

LOCATION • ____________________ *Date* • / /

Attendees •

Notes •

Total • $ __________

LOCATION • ____________________ *Date* • / /

Attendees •

Notes •

Total • $ __________

LOCATION • ____________________ *Date* • / /

Attendees •

Notes •

Total • $ __________

LOCATION • ____________________ *Date* • / /

Attendees •

Notes •

Total • $ __________

LOCATION • ____________________ *Date* • / /

Attendees •

Notes •

Total • $ __________

LOCATION • ______________________ Date • / /

Attendees •

Notes •

Total • $ __________

LOCATION • ______________________ Date • / /

Attendees •

Notes •

Total • $ __________

LOCATION • ______________________ Date • / /

Attendees •

Notes •

Total • $ __________

LOCATION • ______________________ Date • / /

Attendees •

Notes •

Total • $ __________

LOCATION • ______________________ Date • / /

Attendees •

Notes •

Total • $ __________

LOCATION • ____________________ *Date* • / /

Attendees •

Notes •

Total • $ __________

LOCATION • ____________________ *Date* • / /

Attendees •

Notes •

Total • $ __________

LOCATION • ____________________ *Date* • / /

Attendees •

Notes •

Total • $ __________

LOCATION • ____________________ *Date* • / /

Attendees •

Notes •

Total • $ __________

LOCATION • ____________________ *Date* • / /

Attendees •

Notes •

Total • $ __________

LOCATION • ____________________ Date • / /

Attendees •

Notes •

Total • $ __________

LOCATION • ____________________ Date • / /

Attendees •

Notes •

Total • $ __________

LOCATION • ____________________ Date • / /

Attendees •

Notes •

Total • $ __________

LOCATION • ____________________ Date • / /

Attendees •

Notes •

Total • $ __________

LOCATION • ____________________ Date • / /

Attendees •

Notes •

Total • $ __________

TRAVEL, ENTERTAINMENT, & MEALS

LOCATION • ____________________ *Date* • / /

Attendees •

Notes •

Total • $ __________

LOCATION • ____________________ *Date* • / /

Attendees •

Notes •

Total • $ __________

LOCATION • ____________________ *Date* • / /

Attendees •

Notes •

Total • $ __________

LOCATION • ____________________ *Date* • / /

Attendees •

Notes •

Total • $ __________

LOCATION • ____________________ *Date* • / /

Attendees •

Notes •

Total • $ __________

UNREIMBURSED BUSINESS EXPENSE

An expense that is common to your trade or business but which is not reimbursed by an employer or contractor may be tax deductible. In order to qualify, the expense must be appropriate and helpful to your work, or be required as a condition of your employment or for the convenience of your employer. This includes unreimbursed expenses for business-related travel and education, as well as the expenses associated with a home office. In most cases, the costs are deductible as a miscellaneous expense after you have met the deduction threshold of 2% of your AGI.

EXPENSES WHICH MAY BE DEDUCTIBLE

Tax deductible examples of direct expenses of the home office or home workspace include **equipment**, such as computers and their peripherals, telephones, PDAs, fax machines, copiers, telephones, audio equipment, furniture and furnishings, software, vehicles, and tools that are specific to your trade.

Supplies that are used in your trade or business are tax deductible, for example, bar supplies, kitchen items, batteries, publications, paper goods, cleaning supplies, ink cartridges and toner, disks, calendars and coffee. **Clothing and uniform** costs are tax deductible if the items are protective in nature, specially designed, and not adaptable for everyday wear. This deduction includes uniforms or articles of clothing displaying an employer's logo or advertising. The cost to purchase, clean, and maintain the clothing may also be deducted.

Unreimbursed **advertising costs** associated with business activity are tax deductible. This can include business cards, yellow pages listings, and other ads. The cost of **membership** in professional associations, community booster clubs, and chambers of commerce is tax deductible if it promotes your work or membership can help you carry out the duties of your job.

Miscellaneous business expenses are tax deductible if they are not reimbursed by an employer and are appropriate and necessary or helpful to your trade or business. A wide variety of expenses are included, for example, union dues, holiday tips, gifts to associates, passports, moving expenses, and postage.

DATE	ITEM
/ /	
/ /	
/ /	
/ /	
/ /	
/ /	
/ /	
/ /	
/ /	
/ /	
/ /	
/ /	
/ /	
/ /	
/ /	
/ /	
/ /	
/ /	
/ /	
/ /	
/ /	
/ /	
/ /	
/ /	

UNREIMBURSED BUSINESS EXPENSE

AMOUNT	*PURPOSE*	√
		☐
		☐
		☐
		☐
		☐
		☐
		☐
		☐
		☐
		☐
		☐
		☐
		☐
		☐
		☐
		☐
		☐
		☐
		☐
		☐
		☐
		☐
		☐
		☐

DATE	ITEM
/ /	
/ /	
/ /	
/ /	
/ /	
/ /	
/ /	
/ /	
/ /	
/ /	
/ /	
/ /	
/ /	
/ /	
/ /	
/ /	
/ /	
/ /	
/ /	
/ /	
/ /	
/ /	
/ /	
/ /	

UNREIMBURSED BUSINESS EXPENSE

AMOUNT	*PURPOSE*	√
		☐
		☐
		☐
		☐
		☐
		☐
		☐
		☐
		☐
		☐
		☐
		☐
		☐
		☐
		☐
		☐
		☐
		☐
		☐
		☐
		☐
		☐
		☐
		☐

DATE	ITEM
/ /	
/ /	
/ /	
/ /	
/ /	
/ /	
/ /	
/ /	
/ /	
/ /	
/ /	
/ /	
/ /	
/ /	
/ /	
/ /	
/ /	
/ /	
/ /	
/ /	
/ /	
/ /	
/ /	
/ /	

UNREIMBURSED BUSINESS EXPENSE

AMOUNT	*PURPOSE*	√
		☐
		☐
		☐
		☐
		☐
		☐
		☐
		☐
		☐
		☐
		☐
		☐
		☐
		☐
		☐
		☐
		☐
		☐
		☐
		☐
		☐
		☐
		☐
		☐

CHARITABLE CONTRIBUTIONS

Charitable contributions are tax deductible if made by an individual or corporation to an IRS-approved, tax-exempt nonprofit organization. Other partnerships, sole proprietorships, and limited liability corporations are not eligible for this deduction. Eligible tax-exempt nonprofit organizations include charitable or religious entities, fraternal lodges, veterans' organizations, legal service corporations, and agencies of the U.S. or Indian tribal governments.

Contributions to political organizations and political candidates may not be deducted.

A contribution of fully-depreciated assets is not tax deductible. Individuals can not claim a deduction for the value of time and services that they contribute, but the direct costs associated with volunteer service can be deducted.

For most charitable donations from an individual tax-payer, the maximum you can deduct in one tax year is limited to 50% of your AGI.

In the event of larger donations, the portion of the deduction in excess of the cap can be carried forward to offset income in the following tax year.

CONTRIBUTIONS WHICH MAY BE DEDUCTIBLE

Small donations, including holiday toys or canned goods placed in a collection bin, do not require a receipt but must be documented in your records, identifying the items, value, date, and receiving organization. **Small cash donations**, such as those put in collection plates or given to holiday bell-ringers must be similarly logged. The value of **used clothing** donated to a qualified charity is tax deductible. The deduction should be based on either the fair market value of the used clothing or valuation guidelines provided by the IRS. Appraisals are recommended for items that deviate greatly from the guidelines, such as furs and evening gowns. If you receive a book, CD, meal, or other thank you gift for your contribution, your deduction is limited to the portion of the contribution in excess of the value of the gift.

Large donations require more extensive documentation from the receiving organization. When an appraisal fee is paid to determine the value of property to be donated to a qualified charity, that fee is tax deductible.

If you donate your **used personal car** to a qualified charity the deduction is limited to the fair market value of the vehicle. The published "blue book" value is no longer accepted as a method of valuation for tax purposes. If the receiving organization sells or otherwise disposes of the car, the amount it receives is an acceptable valuation. In most cases, a qualified appraisal is suggested.

The value of **real estate** donated for land conservation is tax deductible. This includes partial donations such as easements, withholding mineral rights, or donating a remainder interest following your death.

DATE	CHARITABLE ORGANIZATION	AMOUNT	√
/ /			☐
/ /			☐
/ /			☐
/ /			☐
/ /			☐
/ /			☐
/ /			☐
/ /			☐
/ /			☐
/ /			☐
/ /			☐

DATE	ITEM DESCRIPTION
/ /	
/ /	
/ /	
/ /	
/ /	
/ /	
/ /	
/ /	
/ /	
/ /	

DONATIONS

DATE	CHARITABLE ORGANIZATION	AMOUNT	√
/ /			☐
/ /			☐
/ /			☐
/ /			☐
/ /			☐
/ /			☐
/ /			☐
/ /			☐
/ /			☐
/ /			☐
/ /			☐

VALUE	CHARITABLE ORGANIZATION	√
		☐
		☐
		☐
		☐
		☐
		☐
		☐
		☐
		☐
		☐

DATE	CHARITABLE ORGANIZATION	AMOUNT	√
/ /			☐
/ /			☐
/ /			☐
/ /			☐
/ /			☐
/ /			☐
/ /			☐
/ /			☐
/ /			☐
/ /			☐
/ /			☐

DATE	ITEM DESCRIPTION
/ /	
/ /	
/ /	
/ /	
/ /	
/ /	
/ /	
/ /	
/ /	
/ /	

DONATIONS

DATE	CHARITABLE ORGANIZATION	AMOUNT	√
/ /			☐
/ /			☐
/ /			☐
/ /			☐
/ /			☐
/ /			☐
/ /			☐
/ /			☐
/ /			☐
/ /			☐
/ /			☐

VALUE	CHARITABLE ORGANIZATION	√
		☐
		☐
		☐
		☐
		☐
		☐
		☐
		☐
		☐
		☐

DATE	CHARITABLE ORGANIZATION	AMOUNT	√
/ /			☐
/ /			☐
/ /			☐
/ /			☐
/ /			☐
/ /			☐
/ /			☐
/ /			☐
/ /			☐
/ /			☐
/ /			☐

DATE	ITEM DESCRIPTION
/ /	
/ /	
/ /	
/ /	
/ /	
/ /	
/ /	
/ /	
/ /	
/ /	

DONATIONS

DATE	CHARITABLE ORGANIZATION	AMOUNT	√
/ /			☐
/ /			☐
/ /			☐
/ /			☐
/ /			☐
/ /			☐
/ /			☐
/ /			☐
/ /			☐
/ /			☐
/ /			☐

VALUE	CHARITABLE ORGANIZATION	√
		☐
		☐
		☐
		☐
		☐
		☐
		☐
		☐
		☐
		☐

DATE	CHARITABLE ORGANIZATION	AMOUNT	√
/ /			☐
/ /			☐
/ /			☐
/ /			☐
/ /			☐
/ /			☐
/ /			☐
/ /			☐
/ /			☐
/ /			☐
/ /			☐

DATE	ITEM DESCRIPTION
/ /	
/ /	
/ /	
/ /	
/ /	
/ /	
/ /	
/ /	
/ /	
/ /	

DONATIONS

DATE	CHARITABLE ORGANIZATION	AMOUNT	√
/ /			☐
/ /			☐
/ /			☐
/ /			☐
/ /			☐
/ /			☐
/ /			☐
/ /			☐
/ /			☐
/ /			☐
/ /			☐

VALUE	CHARITABLE ORGANIZATION	√
		☐
		☐
		☐
		☐
		☐
		☐
		☐
		☐
		☐
		☐

Following is a listing of IRS publications that can assist you in preparing your tax return. Forms and publications can be accessed and downloaded through the IRS web site at www.irs.gov/formspubs. You can request forms and publications to be sent through conventional mail by calling the IRS at 1-800-829-3676.

GENERAL TAX INFORMATION

When, Where, and How to File........ *Topic 301*
Tax Guide for Individuals........ *Pub. 17*
Record Keeping........ *Pub. 552*
Automatic Extension of Time To File........ *Form 4868*
Change of Address........ *Form 8822*

FAMILY TAX MATTERS

Adoption Topics........ *Tax Topic 607, Form 8839*
Children and Dependents........ *Pub. 503, Pub. 929*
Divorce........ *Topic 406, Topic 452, Pub. 504*

SENIORS

Tax Guide for Older Americans........ *Pub. 554*
Tax Guide for Retirees........ *Pub. 4190*

EDUCATION

Work-Related Education........ *Pub. 508*
Higher Education........ *Pub. 970, Topic 457*
Student Loan Interest........ *Topic 456*
Qualified Expenses........ *Topic 513*

HOME OWNERSHIP

First-time Home Owners........ *Pub. 530*
Home Mortgage Interest........ *Pub. 936*
Selling Your Home........ *Pub. 523*
Moving Expenses........ *Pub. 521*
Real Estate Taxes........ *Pub. 950*

CHARITABLE CONTRIBUTIONS

Qualified Contributions........ *Pub. 561, Pub. 4303, Pub. 1771, Form 8283*
Valuing Property Donations........ *Pub. 526*
Casualty/Disaster/Theft Losses........ *Topic 515, Pub. 547, Pub. 584, Pub. 1600, Pub. 3833*
Rental Property........ *Topic 414, Topic 415 Pub. 527*

SAVING/INVESTING

IRAs.........*Pub. 17, Pub. 590, Topic 428, Topic 451*
Investment Interest.........*Form 4952*

BUSINESS EXPENSES

Qualified Business Expenses.........*Pub. 535*
Business Travel ....*Topic 511*
Business Use of Car.........*Topic 510*
Business Use of Home.........*Pub. 587*
Business Entertaining.........*Topic 512*
Travel.........*Topic 511, Pub. 463*

HOME OFFICE

Business Use of Your Home.........*Pub. 587, Topic 509, Pub. 4035,*
Medical and Dental.........*Pub. 502*

RECORD RETENTION GUIDE

Federal tax returns can generally be subject to audit for up to six years after filing. To comply with the documentation requirements, we suggest that you follow these guidelines for retaining financial documents.

Record | Retention Period

- Federal tax returns.........7+ years
- W2/1099.........7 years
- Home purchase/sale/improvements.........duration of ownership + 7 years
- Expense logs.........7 years
- Banking records (statements, transaction slips, cancelled checks).........7 years
- Investment records (year-end statements, transaction documentation).........duration of ownership of investment vehicle + 7 years
- Home/property ownership documents.........duration of ownership + 7 years
- Home improvements.........duration of ownership + 7 years
- Home repairs.........warranty period
- Retirement plan/IRA/pension (statements, annual reports, transaction documentation).........permanent
- Loan records.........life of loan + 7 years
- Insurance policies.........permanent

Other titles in this series:

Tax Deductions A to Z™

Tax Deductions A to Z™ for Clergy

Tax Deductions A to Z™ for Educators

Tax Deductions A to Z™ for Fire, Police & EMT

Tax Deductions A to Z™ for Freelancer and Contractors

Tax Deductions A to Z™ for Health Care Professionals

Tax Deductions A to Z™ for Home Office & Self Employed

Tax Deductions A to Z™ for Military & Reservists

Tax Deductions A to Z™ for Sales Professionals

Tax Deductions A to Z™ for Trades People & Union Members

Tax Deductions A to Z™ for Writers, Artists and Performers